E. V. THOMPSON'S WESTCOUNTRY

BOSSINEY BOOKS

First published in 1986
by Bossiney Books
St Teath, Bodmin, Cornwall
Printed and bound in Great Britain by
A. Wheaton & Co. Ltd, Exeter

All Rights Reserved
© E. V. Thompson 1986
ISBN 0 948158 23 9

Plate Acknowledgments
Front and Back covers by Ray Bishop
Old Picture Postcards: Peter Bray
Rosemary Clinch: pages 6, 14–18 lower, 20, 21, 23, 26, 27 lower, 30, 31 lower, 35 upper
Ray Bishop: pages 3, 12, 13 lower, 55, 57, 59, 61–63, 67–70, 72, 74 upper, 79, 80, 82–85 lower, 88, 90, 93, 94
Ken Duxbury: pages 4/5, 9, 13 upper, 37, 54, 64, 65, 73, 76, 77, 81, 89, 92
Mark Bygrave: pages 7, 10, 22, 31 upper, 32, 40, 41 upper, 49
Michael Deering: pages 24, 25, 28, 33
David C. Golby: pages 1, 44, 45, 53
Alice Boyd: page 87 upper
Roy J. Westlake: pages 8, 52
George Gallop: page 18 upper
John Harvey & Sons Ltd: page 19
Julia Davey: page 27 upper
Peter Friend: page 29
Fleet Air Arm Museum, Yeovilton: pages 34, 35 lower
BRNC Dartmouth: page 42
Mark S. Wilkins: page 43
Marylou North: page 56
C. & S. Clemens: page 71 right
David Clarke: page 78
English China Clay Group: page 85 upper
Cornwall Aero Park: page 91

Front cover: Heather Swain on the North Cornish Coast
Back cover: On Roughtor, Bodmin Moor

The author with his portrait and the artist, Nicholas St John Rosse, in the St Nectan's Glen studio of this very talented painter. St John Rosse was a pupil of Annigoni in his Florence studio for three years. Since then he has exhibited in many major centres around the world.

Cornwall has known many fine painters over the years. The eighteenth-century portrait painter John Opie from St Agnes was one of Cornwall's own sons. Others who have lived or painted here include Whistler, Sickert and Stanhope Forbes, to name but a few.

INTRODUCING E. V. THOMPSON – AND HIS WESTCOUNTRY

Cornwall has a great tradition of story-telling ranging from ancient myth to modern novelists. Dame Daphne du Maurier has written so much here. Winston Graham, the creator of Poldark, had fruitful Cornish years – and keeps returning.

E. V. Thompson is in the same gifted mould.

It was in 1977 that Ernest Thompson shot into the big time with his novel *Chase the Wind*, set on Bodmin Moor. He was then living in an old miner's cottage on the edge of the Moor. Today he and his wife Celia and their young family and various animals remain in Cornwall. They live in a charming house near Mevagissey, an area rich in history which has triggered some of his best writing and is strongly featured in his recent novel *Polrudden*.

E. V. Thompson, skilful novelist that he is, packs enormous action into his stories. Like Ernest Hemingway, he is a master of the verbal photography of *action*. The vivid images, drifting across the pages, make you hurry from chapter to chapter. You wonder when television or the cinema – or both – will start using his talents. In our very visual age, his novels are naturals for the screen – big or small.

The Restless Sea, published by Macmillan in 1983 is a superb example of his craft. It takes us back in time and mood to the period 1810 to 1812. Slave-trading, warfare on the high seas, smuggling, crime and punishment, pugilism, sea fishing and conflicts between the Methodists and the Establishment are all themes. Nathan Jago is the central personality, a young

man challenging with bare knuckles to become Champion of the World. Back in Cornwall, Nathan starts drift-fishing on the south coast – ahead of its time and unpopular. Emotionally he finds himself torn between two young women: daughter of the local landowner – a young lady from another social world – and a fishing girl, smuggler's daughter, a tomboy of seventeen.

BRISTOL. A view of the city from Park Row. This is the city as seen by the author during his years 'on the beat' in this area. Older residents of the city will be able to pinpoint the very many changes that have taken place in Bristol's skyline during the last fifty years.

This is a book surely destined to belong to the top shelf of great Cornish novels, and Nathan Jago, for certain, will grow into one of *the* characters to have grown out of the imagination of Cornish writing. Son of a radical Methodist preacher, Nathan will stand alongside Ross Poldark and Mary Yelland, the heroine of *Jamaica Inn*: memorable people who live on in the eye of our imagination.

Here is an author who not only sympathizes with the underdog, but understands the commonplace – and complex – business of relationships and obsessions. Again like Hemingway, he can show revealing tenderness beneath descriptions of violence.

It was George Orwell who said inside every fat man there was a thin man struggling to be let out. Inside E. V. Thompson, the novelist, is also Thompson, the historian – that second writer at his elbow when he goes back in time.

We, at Bossiney, have been fortunate to have had Ernest Thompson on our list since 1980 when we published his *Discovering Bodmin Moor*. 'To stride out across the coarse grass,' he wrote, 'leaving behind the grey stone moorside hamlets, is to stride back into history. Almost every age of man has left its brief mark here.'

He later did *Discovering Cornwall's South Coast*, a journey from the banks of the Tamar down to Land's End, and *100 Years on Bodmin Moor*, a rich harvest of old photographs and picture postcards reflecting life on the Moor for a century with perceptive text by an author who both loves and understands Bodmin Moor and its people. He is especially at home on the Moor as was confirmed by his BBC Radio Cornwall series: *E. V. Thompson's Moor*.

It is with pleasure that we now present *E. V. Thompson's Westcountry*: the triumphant

SALTASH. The Albert Railway Bridge across the River Tamar, one of Isambard Kingdom Brunel's masterpieces. Opened in 1857 by Prince Albert, consort of Queen Victoria, the bridge still carries the main railway line linking Cornwall with the rest of England.

Right: POLPERRO. Probably the best-known fishing village in Cornwall. The close-packed cottages and narrow streets remind us of a way of life that disappeared forever when Polperro was 'discovered' by summer visitors.

completion of a Bossiney quartet by one of the greatest novelists to have made his roots here in Cornwall. Bristol to Land's End happens to be the Bossiney region, and this, by happy coincidence, is precisely E. V. Thompson's Westcountry.

Avon and Somerset, Devon and Cornwall, four vastly different counties – though Cornish Nationalists would fiercely insist Cornwall is another *country*. Grouped geographically they make a fascinating region.

Avon may be a new creation, but it contains truly historic places. Bristol, spectrum of great human endeavour, its streets still haunted by the ghosts of merchants and seamen, painters and engineers, and elegant Bath, where the wealthy took the waters and gamblers lived dangerously, are just two of them. Somerset, though alongside on the map, is another landscape, a varied landscape with Exmoor, the Quantocks and the Mendips all contributing their distinctive patterns. It remains essentially the county of cider, cricket and cheese.

Then Devon: 'English to the core,' as Arthur Mee put it, 'in its fine little towns, its quaint seaports and its hundreds of lovely villages.' Here is the English beauty of green fields and quiet lanes. This is the cradle of great seadogs and Sir Joshua Reynolds. Men like Captain Scott and Sir Francis Chichester have personified the spirit of Devon. Finally Cornwall, beyond the Tamar, where many natives still speak of going 'up to England'. That westerly land of mines and wrecks, smugglers and Non-Conformists, where the legends of Arthur and Lyonesse live on.

The Westcountry, of course, is not restricted by man-made boundaries. It is more a mental condition, a

Left: HELL'S MOUTH. Looking up the north Cornish coast.

Right: PLYMOUTH UNDER ATTACK. Here a dog is carried from the bombed ruins of a Plymouth house. The 'blitz' put Plymouth in the front line of the battle waged by Hitler in his bid to break the will of the British people.

Above: PLYMOUTH. Fishmarket on the Barbican. Sandwiched as it is between the sea and the Rivers Tamar and Plym, it is hardly surprising that fishing has always been an important Plymouth industry. Here scallops are being shelled for the tables of restaurants throughout the country.

response to a stimulus. Truth is it defies neat, simple classification.

Moreover, this is not a guide book – though it could be used as one, beckoning us on, stirring our curiosity. The author, aided by thoughtful photographers, tells us about the style and the spirit of the region, its tone and tempo. He writes from experience that has sharpened perception. He writes selectively, choosing places that have some significance in his own life or are important to the region. The seeds of autobiography may be here.

As we travel from place to place, we fall under the spell of the Westcountry – so easy to fall under, well-nigh impossible to shake off.

But he is not just a regional writer. A policeman in England and Hong Kong, a security officer in Rhodesia's Department of Civil Aviation, hotel detective in London and a civil servant in Plymouth, his novels alternate between Cornwall and far-flung corners of the world, one of the most successful being *The Dream Traders*.

The emergence of Ernest Thompson as an author is a triumph of character, discipline and determination. After working overseas, he returned to England with ambitions of becoming a full-time writer. Twelve months later, broke, but still doggedly working away at his typewriter, he swept factory floors. Then came *Chase the Wind*: the turning point in his life. It won the Best Historical Novel Competition in 1977 and became a bestseller.

Now he takes us on a journey in words and pictures into *his* Westcountry – many of the photographs have been especially taken for this book. He takes us down into Harvey's cellars below Bristol and to the SS *Great Britain* – there is a strong element of autobiography in places. En route he produces some surprises. Who would expect to find him at Minehead? Wandering

around Bristol Zoo ... or at Haselbury Plucknett? Plymouth, of course, must feature in any sailor's journey, from Francis Drake to the *Ark Royal*. He takes us to the Aero Park at Helston, up along the dramatic coast of North Cornwall, and down to Land's End.

Master that he is, we, the readers, are always there at his shoulder. Despite those earlier setbacks, E. V. Thompson, traveller and writer, was really born with a silver spoon in his mouth.

This is a memorable journey.

Michael Williams
Land's End
St Teath

Above: SAILING ON THE RIVER CAMEL. To many holidaymakers this is what Cornwall is all about and the Camel Estuary is a favourite with many holiday sailors. Rising in the hills above the town of Camelford, the river flirts with Bodmin Moor along much of its winding course to the sea. During the Dark Ages and for many centuries afterwards the Camel Estuary was part of an important route between the Continent and the Christian communities of Ireland.

Left: POLRUAN, with Fowey in the background across the harbour. A pretty, harbourside village on the side of a hill, with a fourteenth-century blockhouse, and overlooking one of the most picturesque harbours to be found anywhere.

Right: PENTEWAN SANDS. Even with a caravan site immediately behind this splendid expanse of sand the beach is rarely uncomfortably crowded. Easterly winter storms are constantly changing the course of the small river which flows into the sea here.

AVON

The county of Avon was formed in 1973 by taking Bristol and parts of Somerset and Gloucester and putting them together to form a new 'county'.

When I first came to the Westcountry, Bristol, the 'Gateway to the West', was itself a city and county, a status it enjoyed for six hundred years.

Perhaps the change was necessary to keep in step with a changing world. Doubtless historians will arrive at their own conclusions – and Bristolians have a strong sense of history. One thing, at least, they share with their neighbours in the county of Avon.

When I was a young, uniformed police constable in Bristol many archaeological 'digs' were taking place in the city prior to a major re-building programme. In the boring, early hours of the morning, when a policeman's lot is certainly 'not a happy one', I would visit many of these sites. Drawing back a tarpaulin I might find myself gazing at the crouched skeleton of a Saxon Bristolian, or marvel at a section of cobblestone road of the same period. There were many other finds. Centuries of Bristol's long history lie buried only a few feet beneath the surface of the modern city.

During the daylight hours I would meet many men and women close to the city's history. One was an old

BRISTOL. The Nails, Corn Street. Originally outside the old Tolzey, these pillars were once used by merchants to count out their money, hence the expression 'pay on the nail'. As a policeman, the author once featured with these Bristol landmarks in an advertisement for a certain brand of cigarettes.

man who tended the Cathedral gardens and who gave me fragments of coloured medieval glass. He assured me they were part of an early Cathedral window – perhaps the one smashed in a great storm in 1703, or might the damage have been caused by a rampaging mob during the riots of 1831?

The same gardener also told me the bones of two young girls had been discovered in the ancient burial ground of the monks and contemporary with the burials about them. I have been unable to verify this story so it would be wrong to speculate further.

Those days have less pleasant memories. One evening I stood in the upper room of a derelict house close to the present shopping centre and as darkness approached I watched a whole army of vagrants disappear into the cellars and ruins about me. They belonged to a world far-removed from the bustling Bristol of the 1960s.

There were, of course, those who were helping to build a new Bristol. Men of the calibre of the Irishman I met pushing a barrow loaded with bricks through the back streets of St Pauls at 1 a.m. He told me a very believable story of having been sick and off work. Due to return to work as a builder's labourer the next week,

BRISTOL. The Llandoger Trow. Surely one of the most photographed inns anywhere in the land. Built in 1664, it is believed that Daniel Defoe met Alexander Selkirk here. From this real-life castaway Defoe heard the story that was to become *Robinson Crusoe*.

Above: BRISTOL. Buskers. Bristol has never been short of these colourful street musicians. For many years after the 2nd World War an accordianist who had worked the music halls kept cinema queues entertained with his music. He disappeared with the growing popularity of television, but there has been a recent upsurge in this ancient form of entertainment.

Below: BRISTOL. John Wesley's Statue, the Wesleyan Chapel, Broadmead. John and Charles Wesley, founders of the Methodist Church were frequent visitors to the Westcountry from 1739, and many churches were raised to further their evangelistic style of worship. The Broadmead chapel is one of the finest and outside is a statue depicting John Wesley on his horse. During his lifetime the great preacher rode a quarter of a million miles in a tireless quest to bring the message of God to the people.

Right: BRISTOL. Exchange Avenue. Part of the St Nicholas Market which has changed character over post-war years. The 'Exchange' for which the Avenue is named was opened in 1743 and was the object of great civic pride, the debtors in the city's Newgate Gaol being set free to mark the occasion.

Left: BRISTOL. Temple Church. One of Bristol's most interesting ruins, with a tower that leans at an angle reminiscent of Pisa. The foundations began to sink when the tower was being heightened in the Middle Ages, but it still stands although the church itself was gutted by German bombs during the 2nd World War. However, the bells still call the faithful to prayer, having been removed to the cathedral some years ago.

Left: BRISTOL. The SS *Great Britain*. Another example of the genius of I.K. Brunel. This was the largest ship in the world when the keel was laid in Bristol on 19 July 1839. It was also a revolutionary design. Steam was not yet universally accepted, their Lordships of the Admiralty seemingly determined to retain ships of the type which served Great Britain at Trafalgar. Brunel's passenger ship was not only driven by steam, but was made of *iron* and driven by a *propellor*! History proved Brunel to be right. The career of the SS *Great Britain* is a remarkable one. So too is the story of the vessel's return to its birthplace from the Falkland Islands where it had been a hulk since 1886. Work is still being carried out on this remarkable vessel, but much of the former glory has been restored and the ship's presence here is a tribute to Brunel – and to Bristol.

Right: BRISTOL. The Lord Mayor's Chapel. Owned not by the Church but by the City Corporation, this fascinating old church dates from the thirteenth century and an interesting series of gargoyles decorates the outside walls. The Chapel has witnessed much pomp and ceremony occasioned by the arrival of the Judges of Assize in the city.

BRISTOL. Harveys of Bristol. The Unicorn Inn is the final call for visitors who tour the Wine Museum. The furnishings date from the sixteenth century, long before the Harveys gained their reputation as fearless merchant seamen. In sharp contrast to his ancestors, the man who gave his name to the family business was terrified by the thought of putting to sea. Instead, John Harvey put his undoubted talents towards making 'John Harvey & Sons' one of the most respected names in the world of fine wines.

BRISTOL ZOO. Polar bears. This is a very fine zoo indeed, with an excellent breeding record. The Bristol Clifton and West of England Zoological Society came into being in September, 1835 and among its founders was that busiest of men, Isambard Kingdom Brunel. For many years one of the most famous animals in the zoo was Alfred, the gorilla. After his death, he gained a place as an exhibit in the Bristol museum.

doubts had come to him in the middle of the night about his fitness for such arduous work. ... 'No strength in me wrists, d'you see?' A man of action, he had leaped from his bed and headed for the nearest building site. Loading the wheelbarrow, he was now wheeling it around the block a few times ... 'For the wrists, you understand?'

I admired the Irishman's determination to give his prospective employer value for money. An hour or so later I was expressing equal admiration for the 12 feet-high garden wall he was building for his landlord from bricks stolen from the building site.

Such ingenuity would have been appreciated by Isambard Kingdom Brunel, the inventive genius who designed the Clifton suspension bridge, built the SS *Great Britain*, and brought the Great Western Railway to Bristol.

But there is far more to Avon than a single city. A few miles to the south east is a city with equal pride in its long history. The City of Bath. Visitors come here from all over the world to wonder at the enduring architecture of the Roman baths which enjoyed an international reputation as far back as the first century AD. The Romans built an entire entertainments complex here, with baths, swimming pool, theatre and temple. The Romans also enjoyed a sophisticated and efficient central heating system. Indeed, the visitor here may well wonder how much progress we have made in 2,000 years.

In addition to the Roman baths the city proudly

displays much of the elegance of an earlier age. The magnificent sweep of the Royal Crescent was at its best when carriages such as those to be found in Bath's carriage museum might have been seen travelling along the city's streets.

Pleasant surprises abound around every corner in Bath. One of the happiest memories of my two young sons is of finding a small cafe by the riverside. Here they were able to enjoy a popular puppet show while parents sat back with a cup of tea and a slice of home-made chocolate cake.

South east of Bath, on the A36 road is Claverton Manor. Here Winston Churchill is said to have delivered his first political speech, in 1897. Claverton is now an American museum, showing many aspects of the American way of life through the ages. Included are reconstructions of the interior of some American homes dating from the seventeenth century.

Some time ago when a jacket was being designed for my book, *Cry Once Alone*, set in nineteenth-century Texas, a question arose about an arrow included in the jacket picture. I telephoned the American Museum in Claverton and within minutes they gave me full details of a Comanche arrow of the 1830s. This illustrates the breadth of their knowledge and a visit to this lovely nineteenth-century house is well worthwhile.

I have mentioned only a few of the places that make up the modern County of Avon. There are many more that have provided lasting memories for me. The pomp and pageantry of the opening of the Assizes in Bristol; the windy heights of Brean Down; a day spent at Bristol Zoo; the thrill of seeing Concorde at Filton; or taking a step back in rural history when seeing the wonderful, old houses at Gaunt's Earthcott for the first time.

This is what Avon is to *me*. There is much, much more to be discovered. Visitors to Avon will go away with many memories of this twentieth-century county. Those who live here will have their own reminiscences.

BRISTOL. All Saints Lane. 'The Rummer'.

BATH. The Roman baths, with Bath Abbey in the background. The Romans established the baths here and visitors from the Roman world made full use of their therapeutic properties. Bath is still popular with visitors from overseas and the city contains much to interest the tourist.

CLAVERTON MANOR, near Bath. It is said the young Winston Churchill delivered his first serious political speech here, in July, 1897. Today the manor is an impressive American museum, containing exhibits depicting many aspects of American life. Its facilities are a delight both to serious researchers and to those who have only a passing interest in American history.

SOMERSET

PORLOCK. A gentle beginning to a hill that through the ages has tested horse, motorcar – and an ancient motorcycle once owned by the author.

This is a county of surprising contrasts and yet, although bisected by a motorway and having a popular coastline, change seems to have come to Somerset more slowly than to so many other counties.

Most of my more memorable forays into Somerset have been on a motor-cycle – invariably ancient – and I have frequently been saved from disaster only by the kindliness of the people I found here.

In 1970 I returned to England after some years in Africa, determined to make my way in the world as a 'writer'. With this in mind I set off from Bristol, heading for Cornwall on a heavily overladen, eighteen-year-old machine. On Porlock's notoriously steep hill I lost my two lowest gears, half my luggage – and my pillion-passenger, and retired in some disarray to Minehead. Here, during the two days it took to acquire the parts for the motor-cycle I spent a happy time exploring the streets and beaches of this friendly little town. In the evenings I enjoyed colour television for the first time, watching World Cup football in the comfort of an inn lounge. I have had a warm regard for Minehead ever since.

Since then I have travelled extensively in Somerset by motor-cycle and motor-car and I enjoy all this delightful county has to offer.

I have always derived a great deal of pleasure from all the many facets of history and at the ruined Benedictine

Right: MINEHEAD. With the tide out. A friendly little town on the Somerset coast.

Right: GLASTONBURY. A place of faith and legend. The first abbey was founded in the tenth century. The ruins seen today are of the twelfth/thirteenth century buildings, but legend has it that Glastonbury knew Christianity long before this. Joseph of Arimathea is said to have come here, bringing with him the Holy Grail, the chalice used by Christ at the Last Supper. King Arthur is also believed to have been buried here.

Below right: GLASTONBURY. Abbey Barn. A magnificent medieval tithe barn where local farmers would bring the dues that supported the monks.

Left: BREAN DOWN. Owned by The National Trust, the headland boasts a field system going back to the Iron Age; the site of a Roman temple; and the ruins of a fort built in the mid-nineteenth century to repel an expected French invasion. Bird-lovers are able to visit a sanctuary here and as a holiday and picnic spot it has been enjoyed by generations of Bristolians.

Left: ALLERFORD. An ancient packhorse bridge, paved with cobblestones.

Abbey of St Mary of Glastonbury, history is viewed through the misty window of legend. Did Joseph of Arimathea come here bringing with him the Holy Grail, the chalice used by Christ for the Last Supper? Did the Glastonbury thorn spring from Joseph's staff? Were the graves discovered here in 1191 those of King Arthur and his Queen Guinevere…?

North of Glastonbury is the city of Wells with its superb Gothic cathedral, the west façade of which was designed in the thirteenth century to display statues of churchmen, kings, saints and prophets. There are many other fine buildings here, including a moated Bishop's palace.

Wells is on the edge of the Mendip Hills, their impressive height dominating the skyline of northern Somerset. This is an area where the Romans mined lead and silver and where early Stone-Age man sought sanctuary in the caves of Cheddar Gorge eight thousand years before the feet of Roman legions trod the turf of England.

Right: EXMOOR. TARR STEPS. It has been claimed that this is the oldest bridge in England – although it was believed in earlier times that the stones were placed here by the Devil, someone even claiming to have seen a cat disappear in a cloud of sulphuric smoke whilst crossing the bridge! More certain is the fact that people have used the stones to cross the River Barle for more than 2,000 years.

The rider in the photograph is Bossiney author, journalist and television presenter, Sally Jones.

Left: TAUNTON. Bridge over the River Tone. The Somerset County Museum is housed in the twelfth-century castle, once a stronghold of the Bishops of Winchester.

I have referred to Somerset as a county of contrasts and only a few miles from the heights of the Mendips are the mudflats of the Bridgwater Bay Nature Reserve where it is possible to see a delightful array of sea-shore birds. Among them are white-fronted geese, shelduck, and a wide variety of waders. Nearby is a historic building of the future – the nuclear power station at Hinckley Point.

Inland from Bridgwater Bay is the small village of Nether Stowey. Here the young poet Samuel Taylor Coleridge lived for three years with his wife. It was an unhappy marriage, yet Coleridge was still able to write such lines as these, taken from his poem, 'Frost at Midnight':

Left: BRIDGWATER. The River Parrett gives an air of tranquillity to this busy little town. Robert Blake, one of Britain's greatest admirals was born here, and his statue presides over the town centre. A staunch Parliamentarian during the Civil War, Blake destroyed the Royalist fleet and inflicted crushing defeats on the Dutch and Spanish navies. His exploits earned him a state funeral in Westminster, but when King Charles returned to England to take up the throne he had Blake's body exhumed and flung into a pit.

Right: NETHER STOWEY. Coleridge's Cottage. The young poet lived here with his wife and small son for three years from 1796. Here inspiration for his poem, *Kubla Khan*, came to him in a dream. Here, too, he wrote *The Rime of the Ancient Mariner*, perhaps the most famous of his poems.

… The inmates of my cottage, all at rest,
Have left me to that solitude, which suits
Abstruser musings: save that at my side
My cradled infant slumbers peacefully
'Tis calm indeed! So calm that it disturbs …

Far to the south of the county, not so far from the Dorset border is the small village of Haselbury Plucknett. I paid a visit here hoping to learn something of my wife's Plucknett ancestors. I learned little, but for those wishing to enjoy the quiet of a small village church a visit to Haselbury Plucknett will not be wasted.

Right: HASELBURY PLUCKNETT Church. The name is that of one of William the Conqueror's knights who came with him from Normandy and helped him conquer the British Isles.

Above: CHEDDAR GORGE. This spectacular beauty spot is a cradle of civilisation. A skeleton found in Gough's cave, and now on view in the adjacent museum, is thought to be that of a man who died a violent death here some 10,000 years ago. Visitors come from all over the world to see the caves with their wonderful collections of stalactites and stalagmites.

Right: SWEETWORTHY. This waterfall is another of the many attractive features of Exmoor.

YEOVILTON. Royal Naval Air Station. *Left:* Prince Andrew, Royal Naval helicopter pilot and veteran of the Falkland Islands war, is photographed here with his crew.

Prince Charles also flew here during his naval days and after making his first flight under instruction in a Wessex 5 helicopter he was described as 'a natural pilot' by the Air Correspondent of *The Daily Telegraph*.

Right: The Air Station is also known in the navy as HMS *Heron*. Open days, air displays and a Fleet Air Arm museum are all part of the Royal Navy's entertainments here.

Above: The Fleet Air Arm Museum and aircraft here aplenty to bring a touch of nostalgia to the oldest (or youngest) ex-Fleet Air Arm serviceman. The museum spans more than 80 years of naval flying.

HMS *ARK ROYAL*, returning to Plymouth on 4 December 1978. A grand old lady with a famous name, she enters Plymouth for the last time, her working life almost over. Soon she will be so many tons of scrap in a breakers' yard. Thousands of Westcountry men, women and children gathered to see her arrival, soon after dawn, but Vice Admiral Sir John Forbes, Flag Officer Plymouth was determined not to allow emotion to overwhelm the occasion when he took Ark Royal's last salute at Mount Wise. 'She has reached the end of her useful life as a ship,' he is quoted as saying. '. . . a ship is made up of people and when they leave her she becomes dead and is fit only for razor blades.

Right: PLYMOUTH. Viewed through the trees from Mount Edgcumbe. Almost three times the size of Exeter, Plymouth has always played an important part in world affairs. Always a strategic naval port, Plymouth has known many great seafarers. William Hawkins, Francis Drake and Sir Walter Raleigh all knew Plymouth well. It was from here, in 1620, that the Pilgrim Fathers set sail for America after effecting repairs.

DEVON

Devon is by far the largest of the four Westcountry counties being some seventy miles from Ilfracombe in the north, to Prawle Point in the south. It is roughly the same distance, east to west at its widest point.

Devon can boast some of the richest farming country in the land, the lonely, unspoiled grandeur of Dartmoor, and a coastline known as 'The English Riviera'.

It was to this 'English Riviera' that I came as a sixteen-year-old sailor, serving in HMS *Victorious*. The ship was part of the training squadron – the other ships were the battleships *Anson* and *King George V*. I enjoyed a glorious fortnight in Torquay at the height of the summer season, but never ventured to neighbouring Paignton where it was rumoured there were signs excluding dogs and sailors from the town's parks! Soon after this the three ships took part in exercises in the English Channel. It must have been the last occasion on which a truly awesome British Fleet was seen. In addition to the three great ships of the training squadron the list included the battleship HMS *Vanguard*, two small aircraft carriers and a wide variety of cruisers, destroyers, frigates and minesweepers.

Devon's famous sea port of Plymouth has welcomed many such fleets home from the seas of the world. During its long reign as a major naval port it has seen

Above: PLYMOUTH. Old Barbican Quay. Fishing boats still bring their catches here and although scenes such as this will never be seen again, a thriving fishing industry continues.

Below: PLYMOUTH. Searchlight display by the Home Fleet. A nostalgic reminder of the days when Britain ruled the waves. The structure in the left of the picture is the old Promenade Pier.

the sorrow of partings and the joy of homecoming. Today the skyline of The Hoe is dominated by a moving memorial to those sailors who failed to return.

It was in Plymouth that Francis Drake reluctantly forsook a game of bowls and put to sea to drum the Spaniards from England's shore. His drum may still be seen in Buckfast Abbey, once the home of Sir Francis Drake.

The Pilgrim Fathers also set sail from Plymouth in 1620, after their ship had been dogged with problems. A plaque at the Mayflower Steps commemorates the occasion and the spot is visited annually by scores of touring Americans.

For some years I worked as a Civil Servant in Plymouth's naval dockyard at Devonport and at the same time was writing my first novel, *Chase The Wind*. This was the novel which won an award for 'Best Historical Novel', a £7,500 prize and the opportunity to fulfil my ambition of earning a living as a writer. I worked on *Chase The Wind* in the early mornings, during my lunch hours and every evening and weekend. I like to think I performed my duties adequately as a Civil Servant during those years. Yet, thoughts of my novel occupied my mind far more than did finding courses for dockyard workers who wanted only to be left alone to get on with their work. However, the Civil Service has a reputation of moving over to make room for the eccentric and the man or woman who marches to the beat of his, or her own drum. Happily, it did so in my case and for this alone it earned my undying gratitude.

Right: PLYMOUTH IN WARTIME. It was not only 'Dad's' army which served King and country. Mums and daughters also played their part. This photograph shows girl firefighters at Millbay Fire Station. Because of its vital importance as a naval base Plymouth came under heavy German attack during World War II. From the ashes of devastation a new city centre has emerged. Some regret the passing of the old, but much of early Plymouth remains to remind the visitor of past glories.

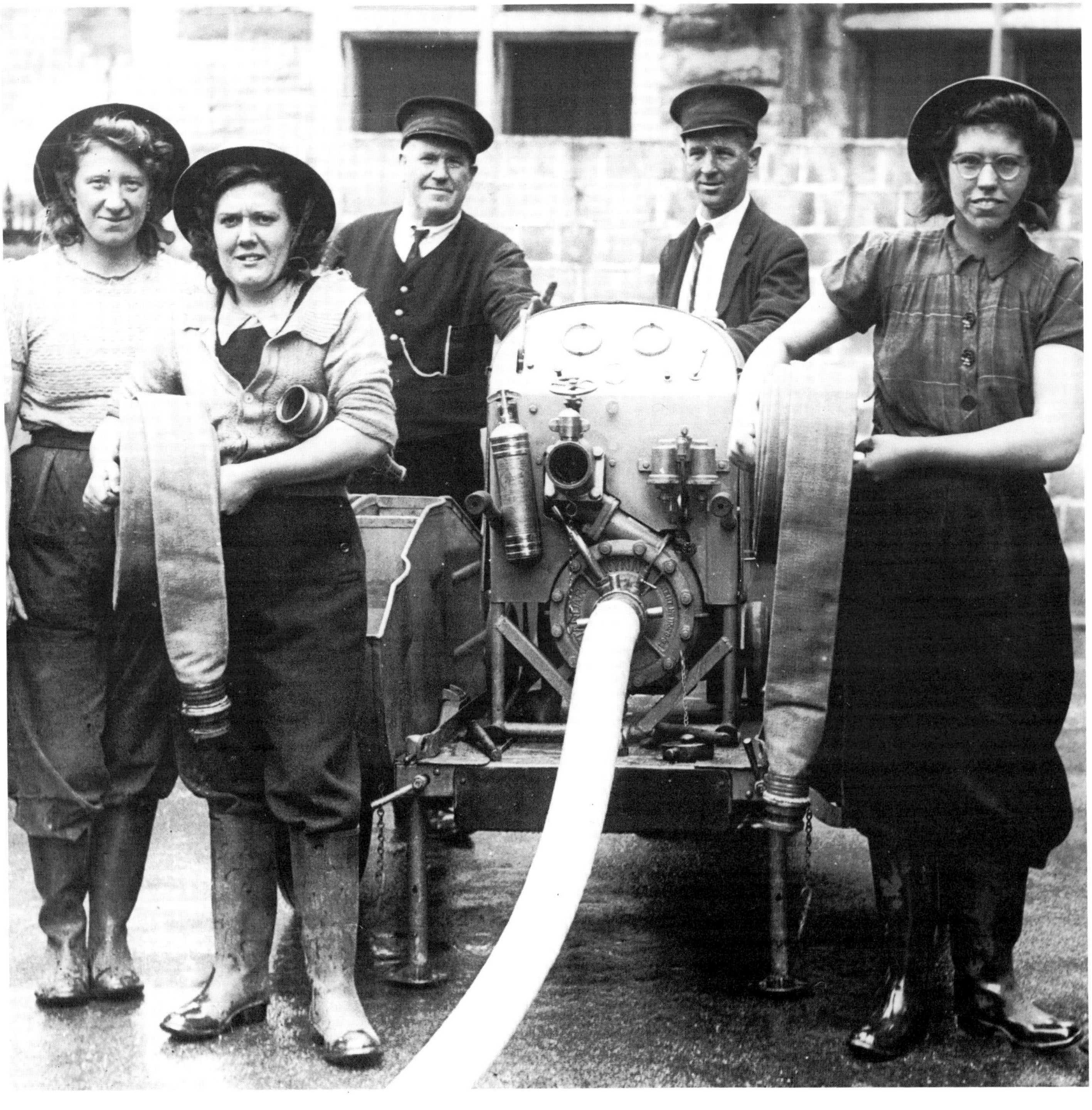

PLYMOUTH. Bowls on the Hoe. Legend has it that Drake gave a game of bowls on the Hoe precedence over the Armada of Spain. Sceptics say wind and tide were against him anyway. No-one would dispute that the Hoe is a pleasant place to be on a fine day. In the background is the Naval Memorial, a moving record of those sailors who failed to make a last homecoming to this famous old naval town.

In my chapter on Avon I have made many references to Isambard Kingdom Brunel and we have not escaped from him here. His bridge still carries the main railway line across the River Tamar to Cornwall.

Devon possesses another coastline in the north of the county, one very different to the gentle, tree-lined slopes of the south coast. Here the cliffs soar to majestic heights and safe havens for ships are few and far between. On this coast on an August night in 1952, the village of Lynmouth was overwhelmed by a raging flood which swept down upon the village, claiming 34 lives. The civil authorities have taken steps to ensure such a disaster can never occur again, but for many villagers nothing can ever eradicate the memory of that night of horror.

Terror of a more acceptable kind was brought to Dartmoor by Sir Arthur Conan Doyle in his novel, *The Hound of the Baskervilles*. Walk on Dartmoor at night, when the wind conducts its own wild symphony and you might be forgiven for confusing fact and fiction.

At Princetown, in the heart of the moor is the grim, grey prison built to house French prisoners-of-war captured during the Napoleonic wars. It later became a civil prison and, as such, it has housed some of the most dangerous criminals in the land.

But it must not be imagined that Dartmoor is a

Right: PLYMOUTH HOE. Smeaton's lighthouse. Completed in 1759, this lighthouse was the fourth such structure on the Eddystone rocks, 14 miles off Plymouth. After 120 years, cracks in the rocks on which it was built caused it to be dismantled and re-erected here, on the Hoe.

Below: EDDYSTONE LIGHTHOUSE. This 1908 photograph shows the present lighthouse, together with the base of Smeaton's structure of 1759, now re-erected on Plymouth Hoe.

DARTMOUTH. The Royal Naval College. A tradition has grown up for future Kings of England to serve as cadets at the Britannia Royal Naval College and today they might rub shoulders with trainee naval officers from many countries of the world. The present college is a far cry from the original *Britannia*, which was moored in the River Dart in 1863.

frightening or forbidding place. This upland moor is wild and untamed and a place to be respected, but it is an area of outstanding beauty and a source of delight and tranquillity for all who come here.

As must be expected when writing about such a large county, I have touched upon only a tiny fraction of its attractions. Many of my omissions are no doubt unforgivable, but they would take up far more pages than are available to me here. There is Westward Ho! where Rudyard Kipling spent many unhappy schooldays; Sparkwell with its hawks and falcons, and where the fortunate might be able to give a tentative stroke to a nervous fox cub; dignified Exeter with its cathedral and fascinating maritime museum; Dartmouth, the college which began in a training ship moored on the river and has dictated the pattern of naval warfare for a century and a quarter ... The list is endless and enduring, but seek such places for yourself. Devon is a county of discovery.

No, not a photograph of the past. Steam lives on with the Dart Valley Railway, operating between Buckfastleigh and Totnes. Here 1450 'Ashburton' leaves Buckfastleigh for Staverton.

43

Above: TOTNES. One of Devon's most ancient ports, Totnes was minting its own coins in Saxon times and when the Domesday Book was compiled, Totnes was the second most populous town in Devon. Evidence of the town's long history exists in the ruins of the Norman castle, the fifteenth-century archway, the Tudor houses in High and Fore Streets, and the Georgian Grammar School building.

Right: DARTMOUTH was making its mark on history long before the Royal Naval College was established here. A port since Phoenician times, it was the Elizabethans who stamped their indelible mark upon this Devon sea port – and something of their swashbuckling swagger lives on.

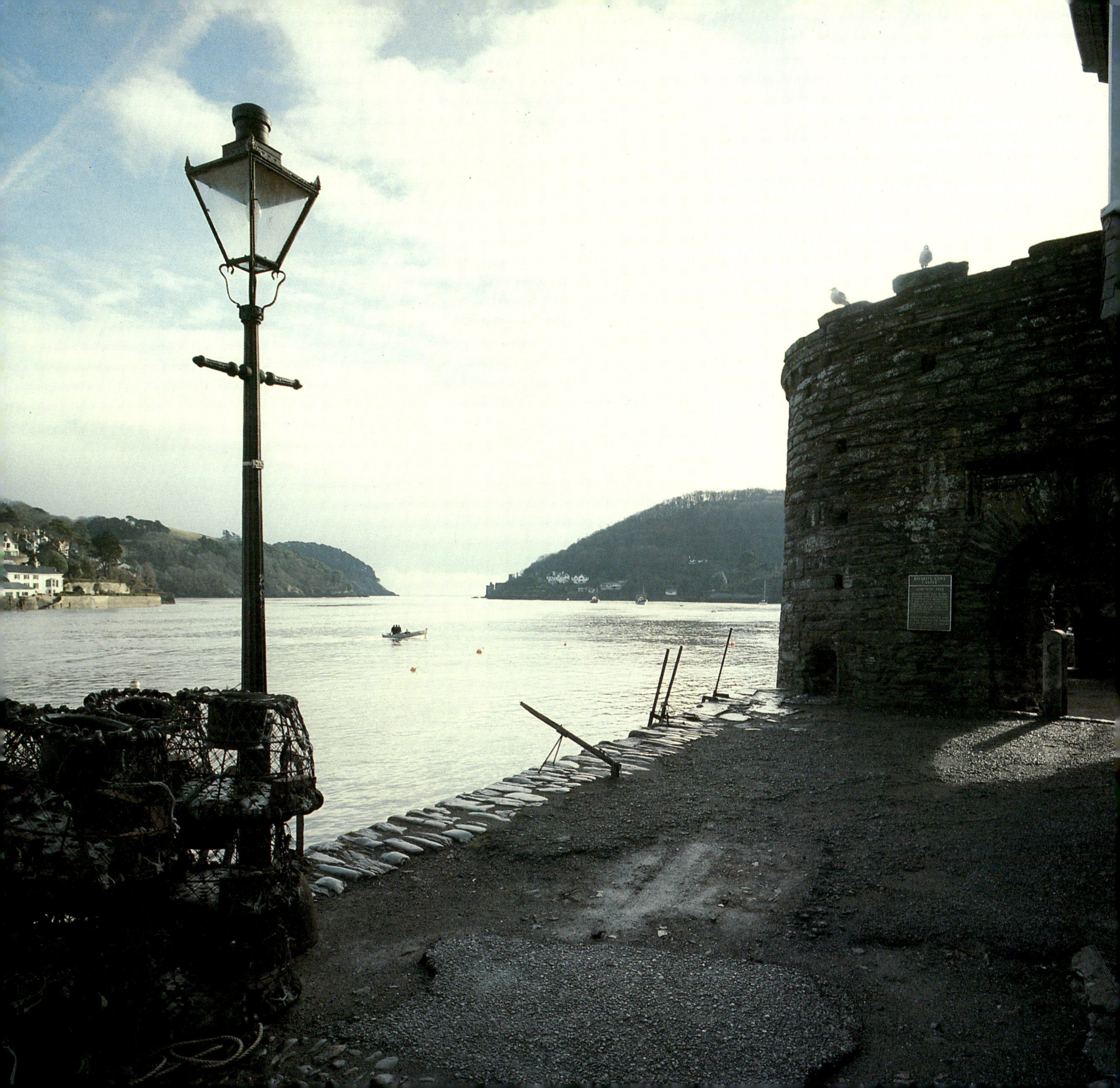

Above: PAIGNTON. A busy day on the sea-front, about 1919.

Above: SLAPTON VILLAGE. Another scene of yesteryear. Now a very popular area with holidaymakers, it was also well-known to American servicemen who carried out exercises in anticipation of 'D-Day', during World War II.

Left: TORQUAY. Motor coach trip to Lydford Gorge. No doubt the passengers prayed for good weather before setting off from Torquay in this charabanc – or were the holidaymakers of yesteryear a hardier breed than they are today?

Above: OKEHAMPTON. Fore Street. A well-known bottleneck for traffic on the A.30, this photograph dates from 1928, when life was lived at a far more leisurely pace – and not a car was to be seen!

Right: EXETER CATHEDRAL. Work was begun on this beautiful building by William the Conqueror's nephew in the twelfth century and it is the only ancient cathedral in England which does not have a central tower. The 60 feet high Bishop's throne, carved in oak and dating from the early fourteenth century is said to be one of the finest examples of medieval woodwork in the land. Drawn by Felicity Young, the Tintagel Painter.

EXETER. Maritime Museum. Here, by the seventeenth-century quay, is gathered a vast collection of boats representing many ages and countries. Among them may be found an Isambard Kingdom Brunel steam dredger of 1844 – the oldest working steam vessel in the world – together with a reed boat from Lake Titicaca, a Chinese junk and many other equally fascinating vessels.

Above: PRINCETOWN. 'The class of '35'. Warders outside Dartmoor Prison in 1935.

Left: CLOVELLY. The main street. Famed for its donkeys, this picture taken around the turn of the century shows how essential these animals were on the steep village street.

LYNMOUTH. Aftermath of the disaster of August 1952, when an estimated 90 million gallons of water fell on the catchment area of the Lyn rivers, resulting in a flood which descended upon Lynmouth, decimating the village and claiming 34 lives.

Left: LYDFORD GORGE. A beautiful ravine, now the property of The National Trust. Nearby is Lydford Castle where, in the words of a seventeenth-century poet, it was said of 'Lydford Law', 'In the morn they hang and draw, and sit in judgment after'! Perhaps something of the forbidding history of the past lingers on because the gorge has been the scene of many suicides. Yet the castle and gorge, together with the church and inn attract many visitors to this beautiful place where the waters boil in The Devil's Cauldron.

Right: RIVER DART. An attractive scene on the upper reaches of the river. The Dart rises in the heart of the moor to which it has given its name. Arthur Mee, on seeing the river fifty years ago, said, 'No British river has a stronger or more varied individuality . . . It has highland wilderness, woodland grace, and the beauty that so often accompanies the companionship of rivers with the sea, when the tide quietly fills the river to the least expectant weed.'

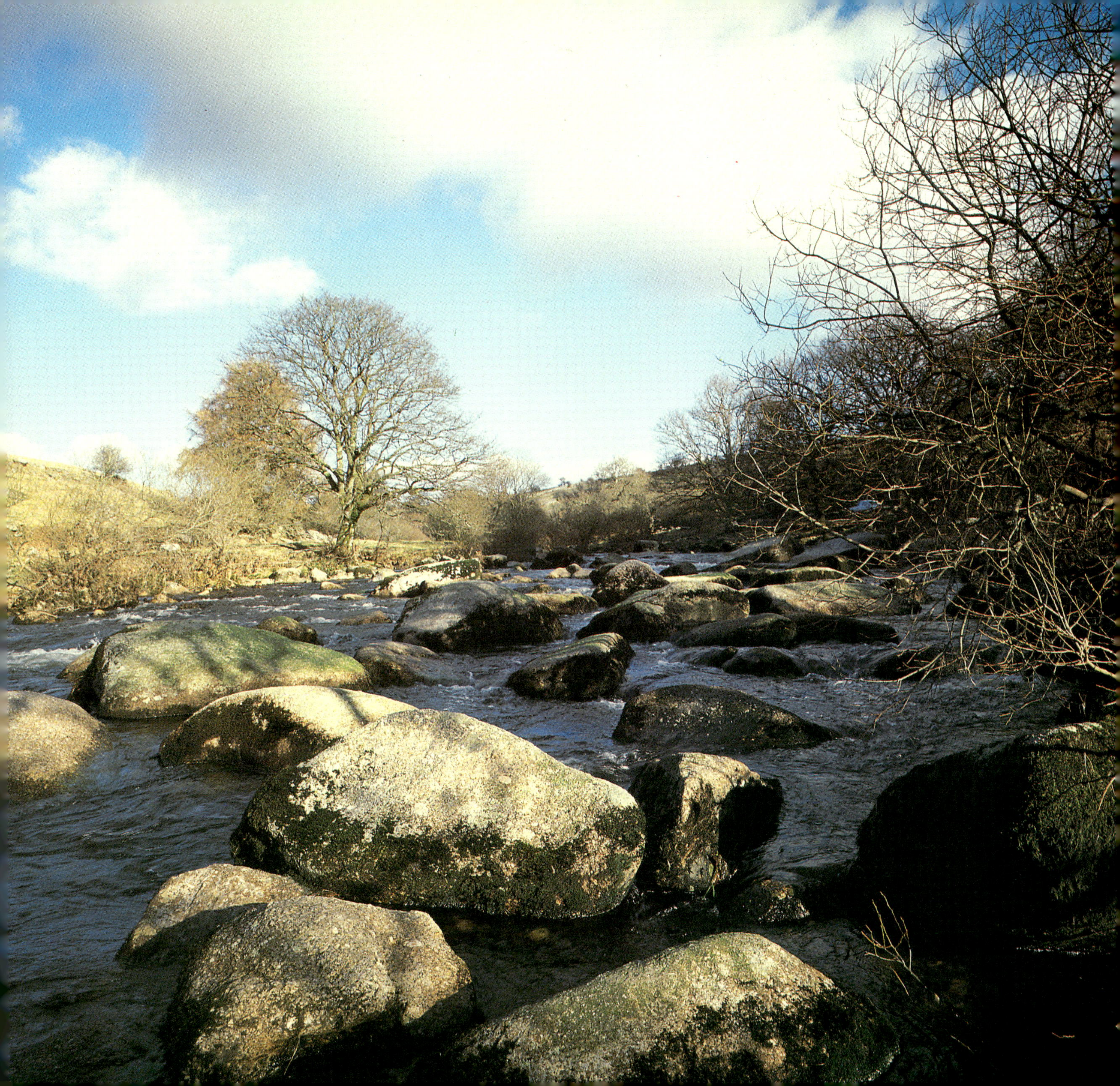

Left: APPLEDORE. The launching of the Golden Hinde replica. Appledore has a reputation for breeding fine seamen and it is fitting that the replica of the Golden Hinde should have been built here. Sir Francis Drake's ship, it was the first English vessel to sail around the world. Other replicas have also been built here, including a Roman galley and a Viking longship.

Right: WESTWARD HO! The Kingsley Statue. Charles Kingsley (1819–1875) was clergyman, teacher and writer – and a passionate champion of the poor. Among his many novels are *The Water Babies* and *Westward Ho!*, the book from which this small seaside town gained its name.

Above: WESTWARD HO! Kipling Terrace. Once the United Services College. Rudyard Kipling was a pupil here, using his experiences in *Stalky and Co.*

LEWTRENCHARD. Once the home of the Reverend Sabine Baring-Gould, who wrote the stirring hymn 'Onward Christian Soldiers', the house was an inheritance. To it the poet/novelist/hymn-writing parson brought a great many treasures, 'gleaned' from local manor houses. The house and surrounding gardens and countryside is said to be haunted by the ghost of Margaret Baring-Gould who died in her chair in 1795, having adamantly refused to meet her end lying in a bed.

DARTMOOR. Bowerman's Nose. Close to the village of Manaton, this rock formation is a moorland landmark. It is not known who 'Bowerman' was, and there is a suggestion that the name is a corruption of the Celtic word meaning 'a great stone'.
The novelist and dramatist John Galsworthy lived on a farm nearby. Best known, perhaps, for *The Forsyte Saga*, Galsworthy won the Nobel Prize for literature in 1932, the year before his death.

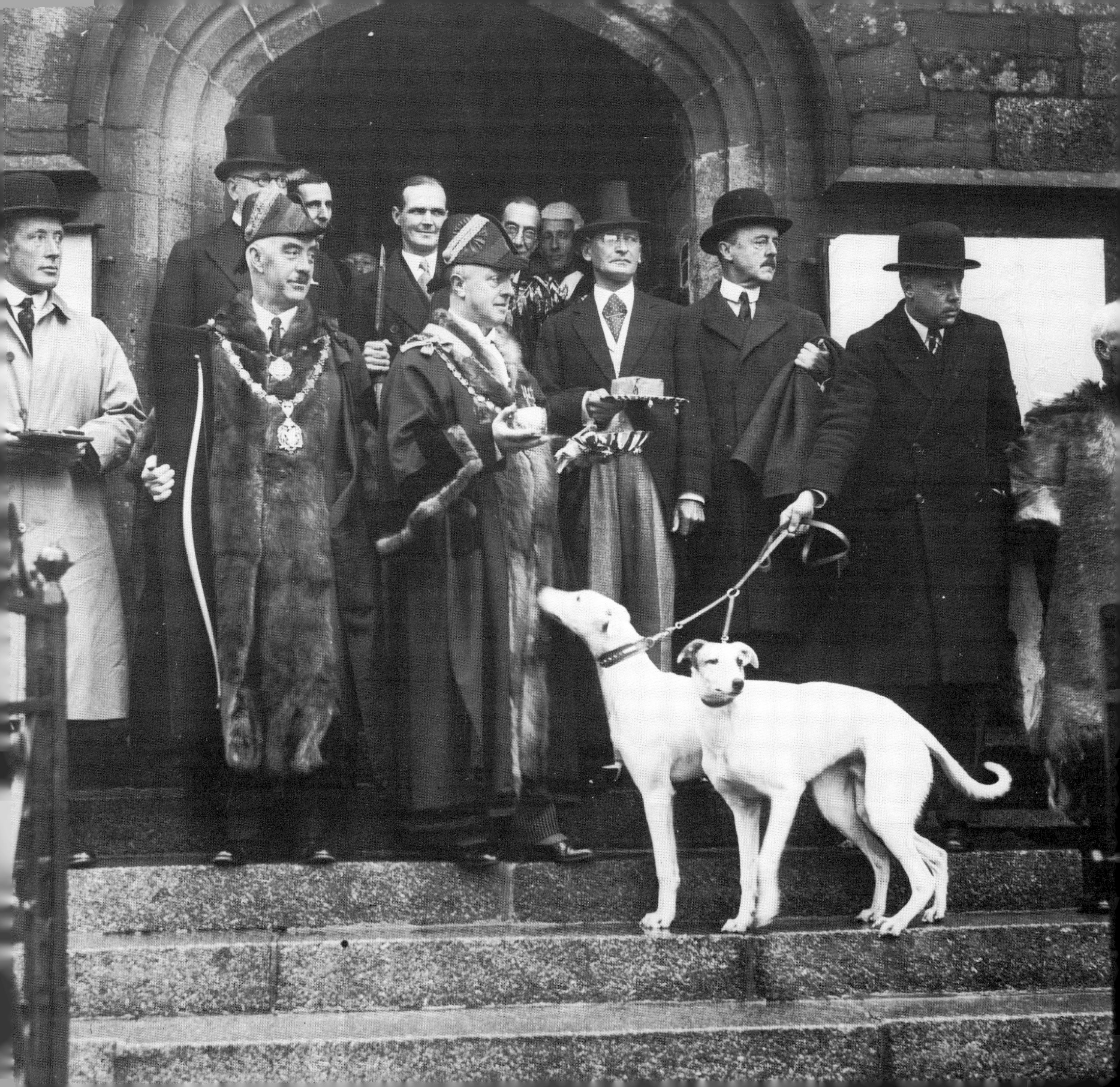

CORNWALL

There can be few counties in Great Britain as well known as this popular holiday place. Indeed, there are times when so many holidaymakers pour across the Tamar it seems they must push the inhabitants into the sea at the other end. Perhaps this is what happened to Lyonesse, the mystery land that legend suggests is buried beneath the waves off Land's End.

Holidaymakers usually come here to enjoy sand, sea and sunshine. While the third requisite may sometimes be in short supply there is enough sand and sea to satisfy everyone and the variety is infinite. The rocky grandeur of the north coast vies in popularity with the sheltered villages and fishing hamlets of the south. St Michael's Mount rises in majestic magic in full view of the whole of Mount's Bay, while Polkerris and Portloe seem to be hiding from the world about them.

The coast draws tens of thousands of visitors every year, yet inland Cornwall has a great deal to offer too. In the very heart of the county is Bodmin Moor, most of it being owned by the Duke of Cornwall – Prince Charles. Here it is possible to find peace even at the height of the busiest summer season.

Not as large as its sister moor across the Tamar, Bodmin Moor possesses a unique, unspoiled charm that is entirely its own.

I first discovered Bodmin Moor in 1972 when I

Left: LAUNCESTON. A wonderful old photograph of Cornish manorial landowners waiting to pay their feudal dues to King George VI on the occasion of his visit to Cornwall in December, 1937. Sir John Molesworth St Aubyn is holding the two greyhounds, while Lord Clifden is ready to present a ceremonial cloak to the King.

Right: LAUNCESTON CASTLE. For centuries this fortress has guarded the road into Cornwall and it was an ancient site when the Normans constructed the present castle. The Quaker founder, George Fox, was imprisoned here in 1656. Known as 'Castle Terrible', the stark ruins still dominate the community that once laid claim to being Cornwall's premier town.

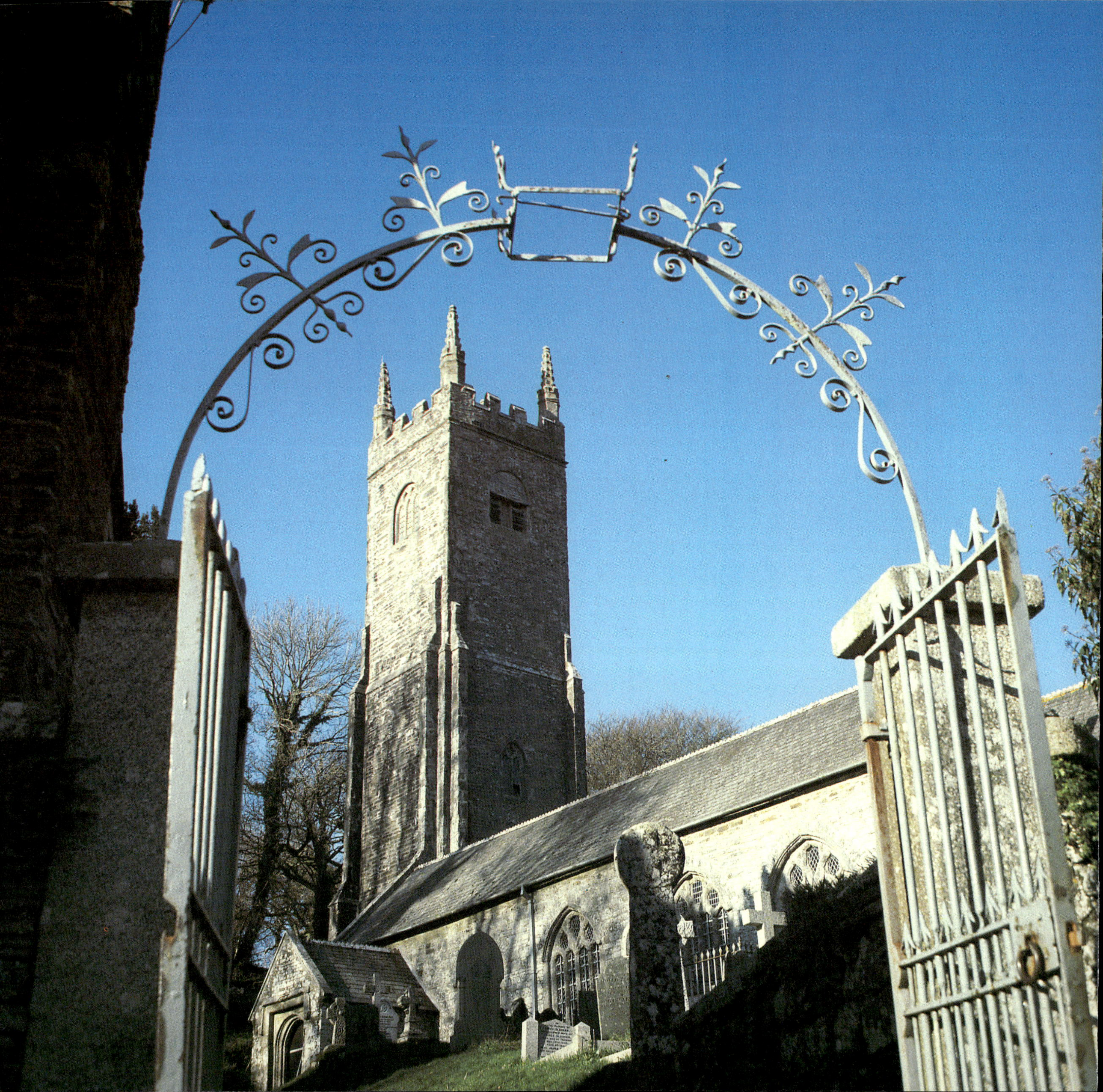

Right: TRETHEVY QUOIT. This impressive Neolithic tomb stands on the eastern edge of Bodmin Moor, not far from the village of St Cleer. Little more than a mile away is a carved memorial with a Latin inscription commemorating Doniert, a Cornish 'king' who was drowned near the spot in the year 875 AD.

purchased a pair of semi-detached 'one-up, one-down' miners' cottages in the shadow of Sharp Tor. Uninhabited for almost seventy years, the cottages, now made into one, presented a few unusual problems. For instance, the overflow from the mine shaft farther up the hill was intent upon flowing through the back wall of the cottage and out through the door. Dustbin lids had to be tied down to prevent badgers from strewing the contents far and wide across the moor. And my ducks ended their days as winter fare for moorland foxes. Yet these were wonderful years. Surrounded by empty, ivy-covered engine-houses it was easy to imagine nineteenth-century days when great beam-engines throbbed at the heart of a thriving copper-mining industry, when the whims drew copper from the ground and pumped life into moorland communities.

Those days have long gone, but the romance lingers on. As I grew to know more about those earlier years, so my first novel, *Chase The Wind* grew inside me.

I have not lost my love of the moor and return there

Left: ALTARNUN. This attractive church, known as 'The Cathedral of the Moor', lies off the main A.30 road which bisects Bodmin Moor.

Neville Northy Burnard the great Cornish sculptor was born here in 1818 and he began carving at an early age. An excellent cameo, completed when Burnard was only twelve may be seen in the Wesley cottage at Trewint and a delicately carved slate headstone in Altarnun churchyard was executed by him when he was fourteen.

At the height of his fame Burnard sculpted the six-year-old Prince of Wales (later King Edward VII), but his work had already begun to decline when his eleven-year-old daughter Lottie died of scarlet fever on 7 March 1870. Burnard's own words in a poem reveal something of his feelings at the time.

Last night I dream'd that I and Lottie stroll'd
At the sweet, tender hour of eventide,
Adown the meads with Spring's sweet firstlings pied,
As in the dear, delightful days of old.

After Lottie's death Burnard closed his London studio and returned to wander the lanes of Cornwall. He died at Redruth workhouse on 27 November 1878, and was buried in Camborne churchyard with no one to mourn his passing.

BODMIN MOOR. Moorland ponies with the Prince of Wales Engine House, part of the old Phoenix United Mine in the background.

often, although I now live some miles away, overlooking the village of Mevagissey with its narrow streets and thriving fishing industry.

Time, like life itself, does not stand still, nor would I wish it so. Many years ago my grandfather left Cornwall and his work on a mine and travelled to London to seek his fortune. He found only poverty. He never returned to his native county and it was left to me to 'come home' – and Cornwall is very much *my* home. As I write, even now, I can see the sea and fishing boats making their way back to harbour. On a clear day I can see northwards to the heights of Bodmin Moor where the raven and buzzard still nest undisturbed by man.

There is the tiny, moorland-edge church of Linkinhorne where lies buried Daniel Gumb, eighteenth-century moorland stonecutter, philosopher, mathematician and astronomer. It is also the church where my older son was christened. The great Victorian cathedral of Truro is where that same son now sings as a chorister and where my younger son was christened.

All these places are part of the Cornwall I know and love. A part of me. For this reason I offer no apologies for making this the largest section in the book of *my* Westcountry. Indeed, I hope you will share my love and delight in all that Cornwall has to offer.

BODMIN MOOR. Prince of Wales Shaft. Even without a roof this is an impressive building. The Phoenix United Mine, of which it was once a part, had a chequered working-life. The first shaft of what was then Stowe's mine was sunk early in the eighteenth century and was given a new lease of life when copper was discovered nearby in 1837. In 1883, two naval divers were employed on the mine to repair submerged pitwork more than a thousand feet below ground, but by the turn of the century the mine was idle. In 1908 the Prince of Wales shaft was sunk and named for the future George V who visited the mine in 1909. The mine did not prove economical and was finally closed in 1914.

BODMIN MOOR. New-born calf. Common-owned moorland has dwindled in recent years, but scenes like this may still be seen at the roadside.

Right: BODMIN MOOR. Young buzzard in its nest on Bodmin Moor. Of all the many birds found in Cornwall, the buzzard is most evocative of the high moor. The plaintive cry of a buzzard circling high above the rock-strewn tors echoes the empty loneliness of the moor.

Above: BOLVENTOR. The Jamaica Inn before modernisation. When this photograph was taken the A.30 road across Bodmin Moor carried far less traffic than today. Many visitors make a special trip to see the Jamaica Inn, one of the world's most famous taverns.

Right: BODMIN MOOR. The Cheesewring. Standing on the summit of Stowe's Hill, this is the most famous formation of balancing rocks in Cornwall. When the mineral railway ran along the side of the hill it would bring thousands of Cornish families here for their Sunday school outings. The moor about this area is still a favourite picnic spot.

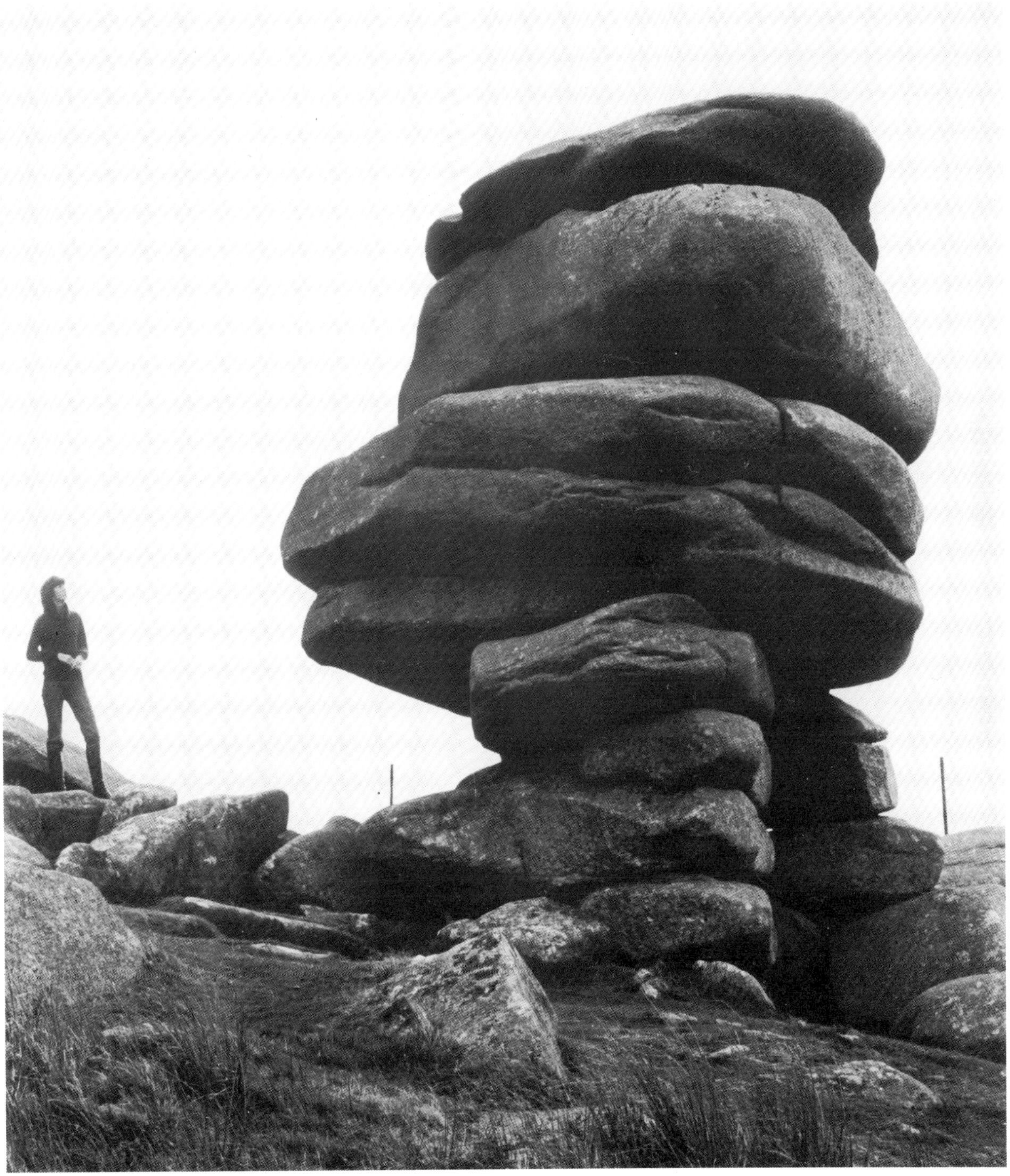

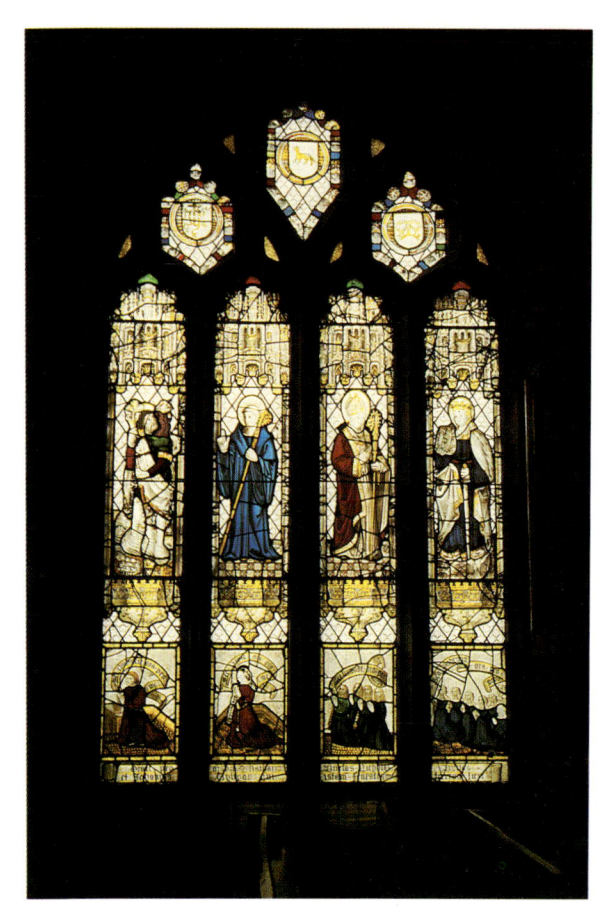

Below: ST NEOT CHURCH. This attractive village on the edge of Bodmin Moor boasts a church with some of the most attractive stained-glass windows to be found anywhere in the country. Legends abound about the Saint who gave his name to the village, some of them being recorded in the church windows. It has been suggested that St Neot was not Celtic, but a Saxon relative of King Alfred. Legend or truth, the beautiful windows of St Neot Church are memorials fit for Saint or royalty – be he Saxon or Celt.

Left: One of the fine stained-glass windows for which this small village church is famous.

LANHYDROCK. One of the most attractive houses in Cornwall, much of it dating from the seventeenth century. Built by the Robartes family, the house was occupied by both sides during the troubles of the Civil War. The house is surrounded by magnificent gardens and the rhododendrons in full bloom are an unforgettable sight.

This is my favourite Cornish manor house. War, happiness and sadness are all recorded in Lanhydrock's long history. Now owned by the National Trust, the house and gardens are popular with Cornish residents and visitors alike. The last of the Robartes family to live here was Miss Everilda Agar-Robartes who died in 1969. Her room remains as it was then and possesses a quality of tranquillity that belongs to a less frenzied age.

Above: BODMIN. Victoria Crosses exhibited in the museum of the DCLI (Duke of Cornwall's Light Infantry). In addition to a great many fascinating exhibits of the regiment's history, the museum has on display all eight Victoria Crosses awarded to the regiment during its long and proud service. The first five VC's were all awarded during the Defence of Lucknow, in 1857. The last went to Lieutenant Phillip Curtis, awarded posthumously for his bravery in the battle on the Imjin River, Korea, on the night of 22/23 April 1951.

Right: BODMIN GAOL. No civilian prisoners have been lodged here since the First World War, but in 1844 an estimated 20,000 sightseers came to witness the public execution of the wretched cripple Matthew Weeks who murdered his sweetheart, Charlotte Dymond, in a fit of jealousy on Bodmin Moor.

Right and below right: Not a holiday hotel, but two very unusual photographs taken inside the grim walls of Bodmin gaol.

TINTAGEL CASTLE. Despite much evidence to the contrary the legend linking King Arthur to this wild headland persists. Beneath the headland is the spectacular 'Merlin's cave' and, in Tintagel itself King Arthur's Hall perpetuates the legend with stained-glass windows portraying the Arthurian story. Legend blends with fact in Cornwall. There almost certainly *was* a sixth-century chieftain/king named Arthur and, given this fact, all becomes possible.

Legends of King Arthur, his castle and his court abound here. Visit this wild, remote headland and you may walk away a believer.

Above: BOSCASTLE, Harbour entrance. This must surely be one of the prettiest little harbours in the whole of the British Isles. The present breakwater was built by Sir Richard Grenville of *Revenge* fame, in 1584. Almost opposite the jetty is the outer bar. Destroyed by a mine during the 2nd World War it was rebuilt by the National Trust with stone from the old Laira Bridge in Plymouth.
Above: The Lady's Window between Tintagel and Boscastle.

Right: LUNDY BAY. There are many fine cliff walks in this area, with views up the coast to Tintagel.

Right: HELLAND POTTERY. Paul Jackson forsook a legal career to make his home at Helland. Here, on the edge of Bodmin Moor, he designs and crafts pottery that is fast achieving international acclaim.

Left: PORT ISAAC. It is not clear whether the lifeboat is being hauled up the hill, or lowered down by the many helpers. Either way, it is a desperately tight squeeze.

Right: END OF THE LAST VOYAGE for a fine vessel. For many centuries Cornwall was the graveyard of dozens of ships every year. In spite of all modern aids to safety at sea and improved navigation, the Cornish rocks continue to exact a high toll from those who sail the seas about her coasts.

Above: THE STRANGLES, near Crackington Haven. Cornwall is a county of contrasts and the softness of the south coast is in sharp contrast to the rugged grandeur of north coast scenes such as this.

Right: CORNISH CRABBER, a yacht designed on traditional lines, off Cornwall's north coast. For centuries the economy of Cornwall was based on fish and tin. Both industries have suffered a grievous decline in this century, but many men still earn a living from the sea and Cornish crabs and lobsters are always in demand.

Right: STEPPER POINT. The cliffs give way to the sandbars of the Camel estuary on Cornwall's North Coast.

Above: ST WINNOW CHURCH. On the bank of the tidal River Fowey, this delightful church is in the most tranquil of settings, with the river lapping against the churchyard boundary. Downstream, where the Lerryn and Fowey rivers meet is the wood reputed to be the setting for 'The Magic Wood' of *Wind in the Willows* fame. The author, Kenneth Grahame, was a frequent visitor to the area. The television adaptation of Winston Graham's popular *Poldark* books was filmed in part at St Winnow Church. Members of the cast are seen here in period costume.

Right: FOWEY. One of the most attractive harbours in the country, Fowey is proud of its long seafaring tradition, although Fowey seamen frequently crossed the fine line that divides piracy and 'privateering'. In 1474 Edward IV, tired of paying compensation to the French and Spanish for the exploits of the Fowey sailors had their sea-captains arrested and sent to London. One of the town's burgesses was executed and the others had their goods confiscated. In addition, the chain which stretched across the harbour-mouth to keep out marauders, was removed. It was poor repayment to the port which in the reign of the previous King Edward had supplied the King with 47 ships for the siege of Calais. London sent only 25.

Today Fowey is a haven for yachtsmen and sailors of many countries who come here to load china clay, dug from the hills to the north of St Austell.

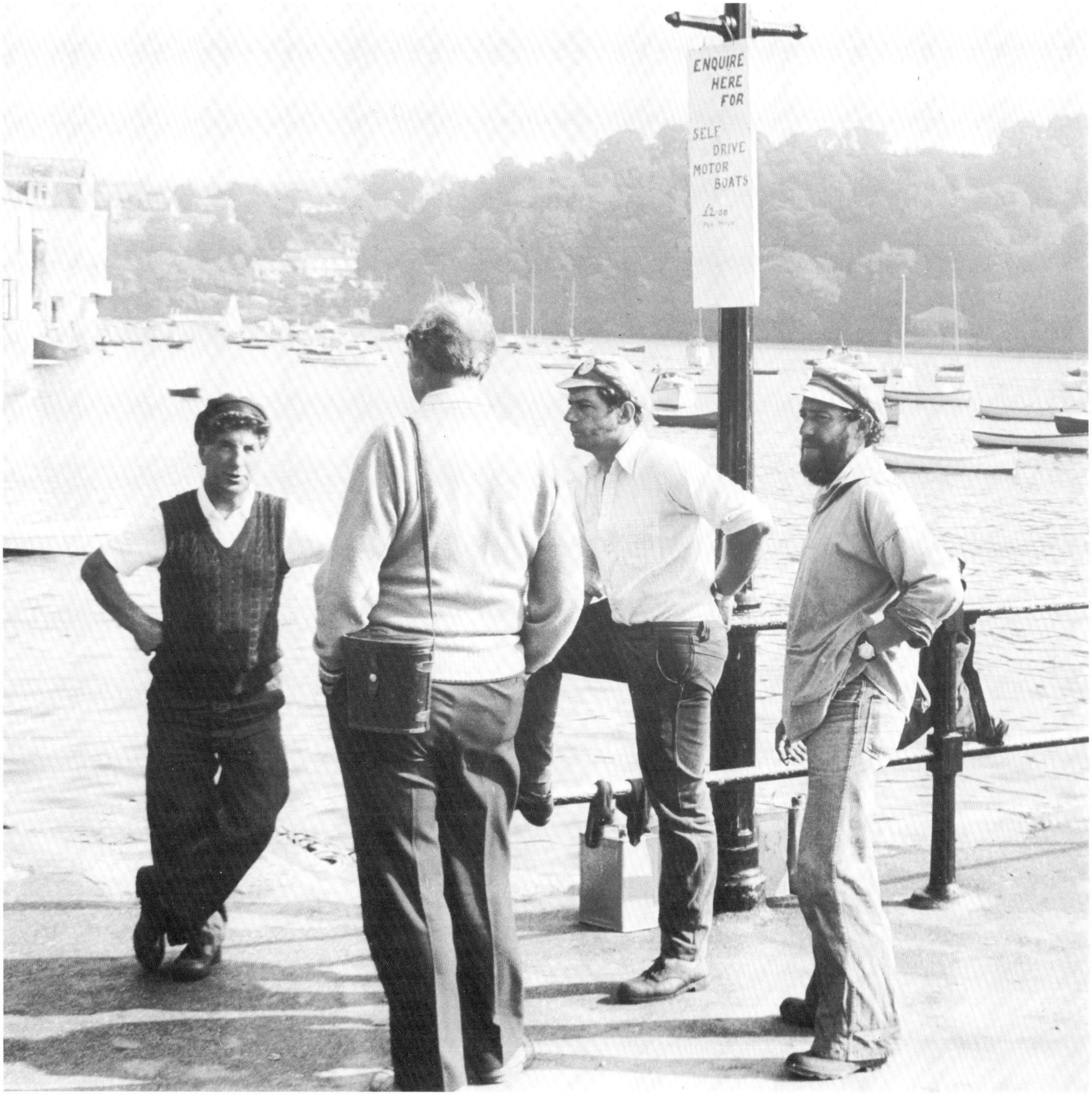
ENQUIRE
HERE
FOR
SELF
DRIVE
MOTOR
BOATS

Above: CAERHAYS CASTLE. The present 'castle' dates only from 1808 and is privately owned. The impressive building was designed by John Nash, more famous for his work on Brighton's Royal Pavilion and the Marble Arch in London. Caerhays overlooks pretty Porthluney Beach, a popular spot for young beach-lovers.

Above: LOOE BRIDGE. One of South Cornwall's most popular resorts, Looe was once the terminus of a mineral railway line which brought ore from the mines on Bodmin Moor and it is still a busy fishing harbour. The pilchard is no longer the mainstay of the Cornish fishing industry but crabs, lobsters, skate, ray, mackerel and conger eel may all be found on a working day in Looe's quayside fish market.

Left: FOWEY. St Catherine's Point. Henry VIII built a fortress here to guard this beautiful and strategically important harbour. The fortress saw action in the seventeenth-century wars against the Dutch. A fine view is afforded from the site.

PENTEWAN HARBOUR. Built early in the nineteenth century in a bid to capture the china clay trade, the harbour was never a commercial success. The silting problem was so bad that a ship entering harbour was quite likely to be stranded here for many weeks. The dock was finally closed when the last ship sailed from here in 1940.

MEVAGISSEY. A village beloved by the holidaymaker. Its narrow streets and a bank of houses clinging to the cliffside evoke thoughts of smugglers and silent boats riding the midnight tide. Yet Mevagissey is a working fishing village with a thriving fishing co-operative and an active community spirit. In recent years the villagers have raised funds to purchase an inshore rescue boat, renewing a tradition which goes back more than a hundred years.

Right: TRURO. Field of daffodils. Flowers are grown on a commercial basis throughout Cornwall and the Scilly Isles. The milder weather of this area means that spring flowers are ready for market earlier in the season than elsewhere.

Left: TRURO CATHEDRAL. This magnificent example of Victorian architecture dominates Cornwall's only city and was not completed until 1910. Built of Cornish granite and Bath stone it also incorporates part of the old parish church of St Mary's.

Much of the responsibility for the building of the cathedral rested upon the shoulders of Dr Edward White Benson, who later became the Archbishop of Canterbury.

Above: PAR HARBOUR. This tiny china clay port, close to St Austell, is one of the busiest ports for its size in England. China clay from Cornwall is shipped all over Europe.

Left: WHITEMOOR, near St Austell. The heart of 'china clay country'. China clay is the keystone of the Cornish economy and the man-made hills possess a certain grandeur.

Left: PRINCE CHARLES, DUKE OF CORNWALL. The male heir to the British throne inherits the title and many thousands of acres of land in the Duchy. Prince Charles takes a great interest in the Westcountry and is seen here presenting prizes at the Royal Cornwall Show in a typical Cornish downpour.

Right: FALMOUTH. Inner harbour. A fine old photograph taken in the days when sail predominated over steam – although there is a fine steam launch mid-right of the picture.
For centuries Falmouth was busier than any port in the land, with the exception of London. In the mid-nineteenth century as many as 8,000 ships put in here during any one year, half of them trading with foreign ports. Falmouth was the country's premier Packet Station from 1688 to 1850, the fast, armed vessels carrying mail and passengers to Spain and Portugal, North America and the West Indies.
The advent of steam changed the character of sea-trading and although still a busy port and town, life in Falmouth today is lived at a more leisurely pace than before.

Right: GWEEK. The seal sanctuary was moved here from St Agnes in 1972 and provides a hospital and convalescent home for sick and orphaned seals, rescued from around Cornwall's coast. Open all year round, a visit is a *must* for animal lovers of all ages.

VERYAN CHURCH at the heart of a picturesque, old village famous for its thatched and whitewashed, round houses. They were so designed in the nineteenth century in order that The Devil might not find a corner in which to hide.

Above: PENDEEN LIGHTHOUSE. A welcome sight to stormbound mariners since the turn of the century.

Right: CADGWITH COVE. A picturesque little fishing village situated on The Lizard.

ST IVES. The Barbara Hepworth Museum is sited in the home and studio where Barbara Hepworth worked. Created a Dame of the British Empire in 1965, Dame Barbara Hepworth died in a fire at her home in 1975. Her work, on exhibition here, provides a fitting and enduring memorial to this internationally acclaimed sculptor.

HELSTON. Aero Park. This grand old Fairey Gannet once flew with the Fleet Air Arm. Now it guards the entrance to the Aero Park which has many aircraft on show and a whole variety of exhibitions and entertainments. Among them is the cockpit of a Lancaster bomber, guaranteed to hold the interest of any boy – and dad as well!

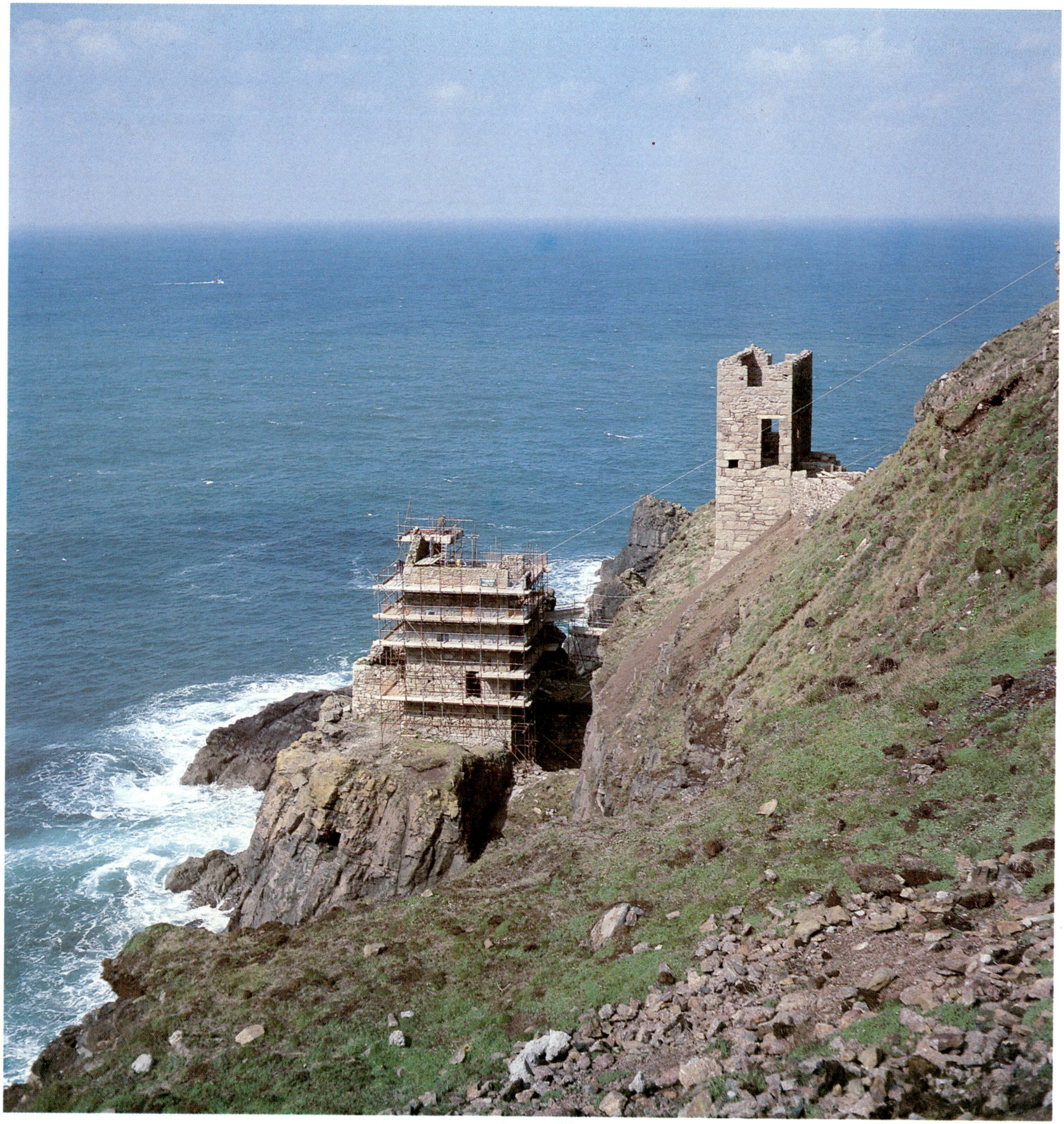

Left: THE CROWNS, Botallack Mine. A shaft from these spectacularly sited cliffside engine-houses went far out under the bed of the Atlantic Ocean. In 1863 the hoisting chain broke and nine miners died at the bottom of the shaft here.
Below: The magnificent rocks of Land's End.

LAND'S END. This view of the Longships Lighthouse has been seen by millions of visitors who come to this famous landmark from all the countries of the world. The seas below the cliffs are unpredictable and visitors are well-advised not to venture too close. A landfall for generations of far-ranging seamen, Land's End and the nearby Scilly Isles have often proffered a cruel welcome. In thick fog on the night of 22nd October, 1707, five British warships under the command of Admiral Sir Cloudesley Shovell were wrecked on Gilstone Reef, on the Southern edge of the Scillies, with the loss of the Admiral and 2,000 of his sailors. In 1967 divers discovered the wreck of Sir Cloudesley's flagship *Association* and many coins recovered are offered for sale throughout Cornwall.

Also Available

100 YEARS ON BODMIN MOOR
by E. V. Thompson. 145 photographs.
A rich harvest of old photographs and picture postcards, reflecting life on the Moor for a century with perceptive text.
'. . . timely that such a publication and collection of photographs should appear now, as a record for all of those who have loved and been inspired by Bodmin Moor.'   Sarah Foot, The Western Morning News

DISCOVERING BODMIN MOOR
by E. V. Thompson, 45 photographs and map.
E. V. Thompson, author of the bestselling novel, *Chase the Wind*, set on the eastern slopes of Bodmin Moor, explores the Moor past and present.
'. . . shows the moor in all its aspects – beautiful, harsh, romantic and almost cruel . . . how well he knows the character of the moor.'
The Editor, Cornish Guardian

SEA STORIES OF DEVON
In this companion volume to *Sea Stories of Cornwall* nine Westcountry authors recall stirring events and people from Devon's sea past. Well illustrated with old and new photographs, it is introduced by best-selling novelist E. V. Thompson.
'The tales themselves are interesting and varied but the real strength of the book lies in the wealth of illustration, with photographs and pictures on practically every page.'   Jane Leigh, Express & Echo

PEOPLE & PLACES IN BRISTOL
Introduced by E. V. Thompson
E. V. Thompson, David Foot, Jack Russell, Rosemary Clinch and Jillian Powell explore their favourite people and places in Bristol. Includes the theatres, inns and churches, sportsmen and characters both of today and yesterday.

MYSTERIES IN THE DEVON LANDSCAPE
by Hilary Wreford & Michael Williams
Outstanding photographs and illuminating text about eerie aspects of Devon. Seen on TSW and Channel 4. Author interviews on DevonAir and BBC Radio Devon.
'. . . reveals that Devon has more than its share of legends and deep folklore.'
Derek Henderson, North Devon Journal Herald

PEOPLE & PLACES IN DEVON
by Monica Wyatt
Dame Agatha Christie, Sir Francis Chichester, Dr David Owen, Prince Charles and others. Monica Wyatt writes about eleven famous people who have contributed richly to the Devon scene.
'A very interesting title from this rapidly expanding publishing house. Indeed, for a "cottage" industry it's going from strength to strength, its territory now covering an area from Bristol to Land's End.'
Irene Roberts, The South Hams Newspapers

WESTCOUNTRY MYSTERIES
Introduced by Colin Wilson
A team of authors probe mysterious happenings in Somerset, Devon and Cornwall. Drawings and photographs all add to the mysterious content.
'A team of authors have joined forces to re-examine and probe various yarns from the puzzling to the tragic.'   James Belsey, Bristol Evening Post

HEALING, HARMONY & HEALTH
by Barney Camfield
Healing in its various forms, the significance of handwriting and dreams, and psycho-expansion.
'If you are tuned in to the right wave length of new age thinking . . . you won't want to put it down until you get to the last page.'
David Rose, Western Evening Herald

DARTMOOR IN THE OLD DAYS
by James Mildren. 145 photographs.
James Mildren is an author who is at home in the wilderness of his Dartmoor.
'Lovers of Dartmoor will need no persuasion to obtain a copy. To anybody else, I suggest they give it a try. It may lead to a better understanding of why many people want Dartmoor to remain a wonderful wilderness.'
Keith Whitford, The Western

PEOPLE AND PLACES IN CORNWALL
by Michael Williams
Featuring Sir John Betjeman, Marika Hanbury Tenison, Barbara Hepworth and seven other characters, all of whom contributed richly to the Cornish scene.
'. . . outlines ten notable characters . . . whose lives and work have been influenced by "Cornwall's genius to fire creativity" . . . a fascinating study.'
The Cornish Guardian

CURIOSITIES OF SOMERSET
by Lornie Leete-Hodge
A look at some of the unusual and sometimes strange aspects of Somerset.
'Words and pictures combine to capture that unique quality that is Somerset.'   Western Gazette

UNKNOWN BRISTOL
by Rosemary Clinch
Introduced by David Foot, this was Bossiney's first Bristol title.
'Rosemary Clinch relishes looking round the corners and under the pavement stones . . .'
'. . . with its splendid introduction by David Foot, peeps into parts of Bristol that other books do not, and I can hardly do better than steal from David's introduction a quote from that great journalist, the late James Cameron, who declared to the editors of the many papers for which he worked, "If you want the facts, you can get 'em from Reuters. I'll look beyond the facts for you." In her own way this is exactly what Rosemary Clinch has done for Bristol . . .'
Heidi Best, Somerset & Avon Life

GHOSTS OF SOMERSET
by Peter Underwood

The President of the Ghost Club completes a hat-trick of hauntings for Bossiney.

'. . . many spirits that have sent shivers down the spines over the years . . .'
Somerset County Gazette

THE MOORS OF CORNWALL
by Michael Williams

Contains 77 photographs and drawings. The first ever publication to incorporate the three main moorland areas of Cornwall.

'. . . is not only a celebration in words of the Moors and their ancient pagan stones and granite strewn tors but a remarkable collection of photographs and drawings of Penwith, Goss and Bodmin Moors . . .'
Sarah Foot, The Editor, Cornish Scene

WEST CORNWALL IN THE OLD DAYS
by Douglas Williams

St Ives, Mousehole, Newlyn, Penzance, St Just, Helston and Mullion are only some of the places featured in this nostalgic book. Richly illustrated.

'This book has something of a celebratory feel about it. Mr Williams, a Bard of the Cornish Gorsedd, has produced a thoroughly delightful volume, packed with a splendid selection of photographs that span the mid-nineteenth century to the present day . . .' Dr James Whetter, The Cornish Banner

COASTLINE OF CORNWALL
by Ken Duxbury

Ken Duxbury has spent thirty years sailing the seas of Cornwall, walking its clifftops, exploring its caves and beaches, using its harbours and creeks.

'. . . a trip in words and pictures from Hawker's Morwenstow in the north, round Land's End and the Lizard to the gentle slopes of Mount Edgcumbe country park.' The Western Morning News

NORTH CORNWALL IN THE OLD DAYS
by Joan Rendell. 147 old photographs

These pictures and Joan Rendell's perceptive text combine to give us many facets of a nostalgic way of North Cornish life, stretching from Newquay to the Cornwall/Devon border.

'This remarkable collection of pictures is a testimony to a people, a brave and uncomplaining race.' Pamela Leeds, The Western Evening Herald

THE CORNISH COUNTRYSIDE
by Sarah Foot. 130 illustrations, 40 in colour.

Here, in Bossiney's first colour publication, Sarah Foot explores inland Cornwall, the moors and the valleys, and meets those who work on the land.

'Sarah Foot sets out to share her obvious passion for Cornwall and to describe its enigmas . . . It is a book for those who are already in love with Cornwall and for those who would like to know her better.'
Alison Foster, The Cornish Times

VIEWS OF OLD PLYMOUTH
by Sarah Foot

Words and old pictures combine to recall Plymouth as it once was: a reminder of those great times past and of the spirit of the people of Plymouth.

'This is a lovely nostalgia-ridden book and one which no real Plymothian will want to be without.' James Mildren, The Western Morning News

RIVERS OF CORNWALL
by Sarah Foot. 130 photographs, 45 in colour

The author explores six great Cornish rivers: the Helford, the Fal, the Fowey, the Camel, the Lynher and the Tamar.

'. . . full of beautiful colour and black and white photographs with a friendly and succinct text from the pen of the well-known author.'
The Cornish Banner

UNKNOWN DEVON
by Rosemary Anne Lauder, Monica Wyatt and Michael Williams. 73 illustrations.

In Unknown Devon three writers explore off-the-beaten track places in Devon.

'If you want to extend your knowledge of hidden Devon then this well-illustrated book is a handy companion.' Mid-Devon Advertiser

UNKNOWN SOMERSET
by Rosemary Clinch and Michael Williams

A journey across Somerset, visiting off-the-beaten-track places of interest. Many specially commissioned photographs by Julia Davey add to the spirit of adventure.

'Somerset has been called the "County of Romantic Splendour", and the two authors have explored many of the less well-known aspects of the countryside and written about them with enthusiasm.' Somerset and Avon Life

AROUND LAND'S END

Michael Williams explores the end and the beginning of Cornwall. Wrecks and legends, the Minack Theatre, Cable & Wireless, Penwith characters and customs, lighthouses and Lyonesse all feature. 90 photographs, many of them from Edwardian and Victorian times, help to tell the story.

'. . . a delightful stroll not only along the lanes but the legends of this celebrated area.' The Cornishman

MOUNT'S BAY
by Douglas Williams

More than 120 old photographs of an area stretching from Land's End to the Lizard with perceptive text by one of Cornwall's most respected journalists.

'. . . a fascinating and exhaustive study . . . It is a guidebook, potted history, pictorial gallery of Cornish life – all these things and very much more.' The Western Evening Herald

We shall be pleased to send you our catalogue giving full details of our growing list of titles for Devon, Cornwall and Somerset and forthcoming publications.

If you have difficulty in obtaining our titles, write direct to Bossiney Books, Land's End, St Teath, Bodmin, Cornwall.